VISIBLE
FAITH

LIVING A FRUITFUL
LIFE IN CHRIST

LINDA BUXA

Published by Straight Talk Books
P.O. Box 301, Milwaukee, WI 53201
800.661.3311 • timeofgrace.org

Printed in the United States of America
ISBN: 978-1-949488-64-7

CONTENTS

INTRODUCTION

When we moved to a rural area in Wisconsin, my husband—who was raised by farmers—was excited to find out the property we bought had fruit trees. And he quickly planted some more. We've got cherry, pear, plum, and apple trees all over. (The peach trees didn't make it.) Imagine how stunned he'd be if he went out and found that those trees had produced pomegranates, oranges, and figs, which were trees we had when we lived in California.

Trees produce fruit based on what kind of tree they are. We all know that. People produce "fruit" based on what kind of people they are. We all know that too. And believers in Jesus display the fruit of the Spirit. What do I mean by that? The fruit of the Spirit is displayed in the lives of Jesus followers as they imitate his life. The Holy Spirit is producing that fruit in them.

So for the next nine weeks, we're going to study the fruit of the Spirit as displayed in Christians.

The section of God's Word that I'm basing this journal on lists the nine ways the fruit of the Spirit is displayed. There are more than nine of course, and this isn't some fruit checklist. These nine are simply a great starting point for a deep dive into how your life looks thanks to Jesus. That said, let's dive in.

The following words were inspired by God and written by a man named Paul two thousand-ish years ago. Paul was a leader of Jesus followers who were known as The Way—today we call ourselves Christians—and he wrote this personal letter to people who lived in a place called Galatia. (Today it's in the country of Turkey.) That's why this Bible book is called Galatians. And here's a little bit of what he had to say:

> You, my brothers and sisters, were called to be free. But do not use your freedom to indulge the flesh; rather, serve one another humbly in love. For the entire law is fulfilled in keeping this one command: "Love your neighbor as yourself." If you bite and devour each other, watch out or you will be destroyed by each other.

So I say, walk by the Spirit, and you will not gratify the desires of the flesh. For the flesh desires what is contrary to the Spirit, and the Spirit what is contrary to the flesh. They are in conflict with each other, so that you are not to do whatever you want. But if you are led by the Spirit, you are not under the law.

The acts of the flesh are obvious: sexual immorality, impurity and debauchery; idolatry and witchcraft; hatred, discord, jealousy, fits of rage, selfish ambition, dissensions, factions and envy; drunkenness, orgies, and the like. I warn you, as I did before, that those who live like this will not inherit the kingdom of God.

But the fruit of the Spirit is love, joy, peace, patience, kindness, goodness, faithfulness, gentleness, and self-control. Against such things there is no law. Those who belong to Christ Jesus have crucified the flesh with its passions and desires. Since we live by the Spirit, let us keep in step with the Spirit. Let us not become conceited, provoking and envying each other.

Galatians 5:13-26

If you're anything like me, you may have skimmed over that passage— especially if you've read those words before. Or maybe your mind got lost in a tangent and you already forgot what you read. If that happened to you (no shame if it did; it's happened to me a bunch of times as I've been writing this!), would you join me in going back and reading through this slowly? Thanks!

Paul didn't write these words to strangers. He wrote them to friends, to people who had welcomed him warmly on his visits as he started churches and preached good news. He ate dinner in their homes and sat with them while they worked. He knew their struggles, their joys, their hurts, their kids' names. Because he knew them well, he also knew the sins they struggled with: hatred, rivalry, jealousy, angry outbursts, selfish ambition, conflict, cliques, and envy. Sounds familiar, doesn't it? He might as well have been writing to us too. And he was.

These words feel so appropriate for our world. In private conversations with my friends, they've talked about how it feels as if the world is getting more evil and that evil is winning. Jesus warned the disciples this would happen when he said, **"Because of the increase of wickedness, the love of most will grow cold"** (Matthew 24:12). You don't need headlines to tell you that Jesus was right. You can see the "fruit" produced by today's "flesh trees" all on your own. You also know it would be easy to be hypocritical about everyone else because the same battle rages in your heart and mind every day.

However, there's one huge difference. And it's that if you believe in Jesus, you have "crucified the flesh [tree] with its passions and desires." Because Jesus took your punishment and gave you his perfection, he's changed your eternal life, which changes the way you live this life. When you are baptized, the Holy Spirit moves in, and you become a "Spirit tree." He starts his work by renewing and transforming your mind, giving you the mind of Christ. This changes the way you think and the way you think about the people around you. You stop seeing others as adversaries but, rather, as people God created, people God loves, people God wants to see in heaven. Then you have the honor of keeping in step with the Spirit, saying no to what your sinful heart wants to do and yes to the good works he gives you the strength to do.

As you study the fruit of the Spirit, please be very careful to keep a clear distinction. The Bible is totally clear that Christians do not do these things to make God love us; we do these because God already loves us. Jesus guaranteed that. And the Holy Spirit displays his fruit in these works. Got it? Good!

For each week, I've set up a pattern that includes quite a bit of self-direction. Why? Well, we are all on different points in our journeys of faith and our walks with the Spirit. The issues I'm struggling with and the growth I've had may be similar to you, but probably not. So having devotions from my point of view probably wouldn't bless you the same way as diving into God's Word and studying, applying, and growing specifically to your stage of life. That said, here's the pattern.

DAY 1: DEVOTION

At the start of each week, my goal is to go back to the distinction above—remembering that **"it is God who works in you to will and to act in order to fulfill his good purpose."** Then you can **"do everything without grumbling or arguing, so that you may become blameless**

and pure, children of God without fault in a warped and crooked gen-
eration. Then you will shine among them like stars in the sky as you
hold firmly to the word of life"** (Philippians 2:13-16).

DAY 2: SOAP MEDITATION

I've been working on developing a practice of meditation. I think I've
resisted it because I always picture somebody on a mountaintop emp-
tying their mind in some sort of woo-woo way. (That is a technical
term, by the way.) When I have tried it from a Christian perspective, my
mind races and I end up making my to-do list for the day.

However, just because (1) other people get it wrong and (2) I'm not
good at it, doesn't mean we can just not do it. Scripture has been con-
victing me lately. After all, King David, a man after God's own heart, is
pretty clear on the topic: **"Blessed is the one who does not walk in
step with the wicked or stand in the way that sinners take or sit in
the company of mockers, but whose delight is in the law of the Lord,
and who meditates on his law day and night. That person is like a
tree planted by streams of water, which yields its fruit in season and
whose leaf does not wither"** (Psalm 1:1-3).

Frankly, if you think about it, everyone meditates. (See what I did
there?) Seriously though, our minds are constantly dwelling on something—whether work or school or family or friends or world events or
our to-do lists. With biblical meditation, we ponder what God has to
say and how it applies to our lives. When we start to ponder, think,
and meditate on God formally, we begin meditating on him even more
informally—day and night.

On Day 2 of each week, you'll use the SOAP method to help you
meditate on Scripture. What is SOAP?

SCRIPTURE: Read the passage or passages provided.

OBSERVATION: Notice what thoughts jump out at you or new insights
you've learned.

APPLICATION: How can you apply that thought to your life today? How
do you live in response to what you just read? How does it give you
joy or more trust in God? Is there a spot where you get uncomfortable
because of how God is calling you to live?

PRAYER: Write a prayer about this truth, and ask God for the strength to live it out.

DAY 3: WHERE I'M STRONG: GOD WORKING THROUGH ME

I love Letter #14 of C. S. Lewis' book the *Screwtape Letters*—and it's led to a transformation of how I accept compliments. Before I read the *Screwtape Letters*, I used to downplay the reality that I have a gift for writing. I mean, we're supposed to be humble, right? Yep. However, if we downplay the gifts we've been given and how the Spirit is working in us to use them, then we minimize the role of God in our lives and miss opportunities to share that he is the Giver of every good gift. After all, as Screwtape told Wormwood, "The enemy [God] will also try to render real in the patient's mind a doctrine which they all profess but find it difficult to bring home to their feelings—the doctrine that they did not create themselves, that their talents were given them, and that they might as well be proud of the color of their hair."

I can't be proud of the fact that I have brown hair. In the same way, I can't be proud of the fact that I have the gift of seeing the world and finding an analogy to our Father. That's just how I was born. (Can I nurture that gift? You bet! Can I choose to waste it? You bet! But I can't take credit for it.) I say all this because Day 3 may be a challenge for you because there's a weird balance between noticing your strengths, being thankful for them, and not becoming prideful.

DAY 4: ROOM FOR GROWTH: GOD WORKING IN ME

His divine power has given us everything we need for a godly life through our knowledge of him who called us by his own glory and goodness. Through these he has given us his very great and precious promises, so that through them you may participate in the divine nature, having escaped the corruption in the world caused by evil desires.

For this very reason, make every effort to add to your faith goodness; and to goodness, knowledge; and to knowledge, self-control; and to self-control, perseverance; and to perseverance, godliness; and to godliness, mutual affection; and to mutual affection, love. For if you possess these qualities in increasing

> **measure, they will keep you from being ineffective and unproductive in your knowledge of our Lord Jesus Christ.**
>
> 2 Peter 1:3-8

Day 4 may be a challenge too. I mean, you know you have weaknesses, but confessing them and getting stronger often requires some work. Can you "fix" everything at once? Nope. That's not realistic. A life of faith is not an on-and-off light switch. It's the realization that you *already have* all you need for a godly life *and* you can possess it in increasing measure. This is not to make God love you more. It is to help you be more effective and more productive in knowing and living for Jesus. This is the fruit of the Spirit.

DAY 5: THREE *R*s MEDITATION

On Day 5 you'll be meditating again. You'll use a different passage and a different format to help you focus. Instead of the old-school three *R*s (reading, writing, and 'rithmetic), you'll be using these three *R*s to help you meditate on the words God wants you to know.

REJOICE: How can you praise God because of what you've read?

REPENT: What sin can you confess because of what you've read?

REQUEST: What can you ask God for because of what you've read?

Along with meditating, consider a *Bonus Meditation Moment* in which you memorize all or a portion of the passage. Why? Let me tell you a story. My whole life I attended Christian schools, and part of my education included memorizing Bible passages. What I see now, with the perspective of middle age, is that the adults were helping embed God's words in my heart. Throughout my life the Holy Spirit has brought those words to the front of my mind at just the right time. Usually it's when life is hard and I need the reminders of God's goodness. But he uses them in happy times too. You are never too old to memorize and embed God's Word in your heart and mind.

DAY 6: SEEING THE FRUIT DISPLAYED IN OTHERS

One of the blessings of being part of God's family is that you and I see how God has given different gifts to different people. We celebrate those differences, build others up, and encourage them to keep using those gifts to bless others. So on Day 6, you'll look for ways that God's heart is made evident and real through a person's everyday interaction. Where have you seen God's blessings tangibly come through the people around you? You'll note that and then let those people know. After all, so much of the letters in the Bible are full of praise for other people shining their Jesus lights.

DAY 7: PRAYER PROMPTS

On this day there will be a prayer provided, but you'll also go back through the week and review the passages. You'll pick one of your favorites and use that to compose your own personalized prayer using the ACTS format. What is ACTS?

ADORATION: What in the passage makes you adore God? Simply list his awesome characteristics and why you adore him.

CONFESSION: What in the passage makes you aware of your sins? God already knows you did them, but it is good for you to admit to the big ones and share the little ones—and apologize for ones you don't even know you did.

THANKSGIVING: What in these words from God makes you grateful? This might sound a little like adoration, and that's okay. It's like the difference between telling someone you love that she is kind (adoration) and thanking her for the specific acts of kindness she does for you (thanksgiving).

SUPPLICATION: *Supplication* is a churchy word, probably because the person who came up with this acronym needed an *S* for it to make sense. Anyway, this is where, based on the chosen passage, you ask God to supply everything you and the people you love and the strangers around the world need—for faith and for life.

PUT IT INTO PRACTICE

I know I've said it before, and I'll be saying it again, but because nagging is also a display of the fruit of the Spirit (it's not; I'm just making sure you're paying attention!), I want to be super-duper clear about two things. Ephesians 2:8-10 says it better than I can: **"It is by grace you have been saved, through faith—and this is not from yourselves, it is the gift of God—not by works, so that no one can boast. For**

we are God's handiwork, created in Christ Jesus to do good works, which God prepared in advance for us to do."

1. The things you "do" do not save you. Jesus has done that.
2. The good things you "do" aren't even your idea. God worked it out *ahead of time* that you'd simply do the things he puts before you.

Your interactions are opportunities to let the Holy Spirit work in you to bless others—the people in your home, your church, your school, your work, your community. Each person you meet is someone God prepared in advance for you to bless.

Throughout this journal, you'll find simple, practical ideas of how to show God's work in your life through your everyday interactions. I asked some friends for examples of how they have blessed and been blessed by others, following the encouragement: **"As we have opportunity, let us do good to all people, especially to those who belong to the family of believers"** (Galatians 6:10). You'll see their replies in the sections marked, "In Your Own Words."

Some people won't understand why you do what you do, which is perfect! That will give you an opportunity to explain yourself. So **"always be prepared to give an answer to everyone who asks you to give the reason for the hope that you have"** (1 Peter 3:15).

LOVE

THE FRUIT OF THE SPIRIT IS LOVE, JOY, PEACE,
PATIENCE, KINDNESS, GOODNESS, FAITHFULNESS,
GENTLENESS AND SELF-CONTROL.

Galatians 5:22,23

— DAY 1 —
DEVOTION

Displaying the fruit of the Spirit is hard.

"Wait!" I hear you thinking. "That is not how the Bible passage goes." You're right. It's not. Yet it's the truth.

Maybe I misled you after what I wrote in the introduction. Maybe I gave the impression that because the fruit of the Spirit is simply what you do because you are part of God's family, that it would come naturally. Well, yes, except that every day is a battle between what you want to do and who you have become thanks to Jesus. And Jesus says that every day you will need to deny yourself, take up your cross, and follow him. And this means showing love to others will be hard.

Jesus told a crowd of people: **"You have heard that it was said, 'Love your neighbor and hate your enemy.' But I tell you, love your enemies and pray for those who persecute you, that you may be children of your Father in heaven. He causes his sun to rise on the evil and the good, and sends rain on the righteous and the unrighteous. If you love those who love you, what reward will you get? Are not even the tax collectors doing that?"** (Matthew 5:43-46).

Jesus knows that loving your best friend is not hard. What's hard is loving those who are mean to you, who mock you, who make fun of you for your faith, who think you are dumb for loving Jesus. And God knows what it's like to be rejected and hated, yet he still sends blessings on everyone—the people who love him and the people who don't love him.

That's why it is absolutely amazing that with the power of the Holy Spirit working inside of you, you can see your enemies through God's eyes. They may be lost and need direction. They may be hurt and need healing. They may be loveless and need to be shown love. Whatever they struggle with, you know they are people who were created in the image of God. In a world that desperately needs it, in a world where **"because of the increase of wickedness, the love of most will grow cold"** (Matthew 24:12), you get to have **"the Lord make your love increase and overflow for each other and for everyone else"** (1 Thessalonians 3:12).

SOAP MEDITATION

SCRIPTURE

For Christ's love compels us, because we are convinced that one died for all, and therefore all died. And he died for all, that those who live should no longer live for themselves but for him who died for them and was raised again. So from now on we regard no one from a worldly point of view. Though we once regarded Christ in this way, we do so no longer. Therefore, if anyone is in Christ, the new creation has come: The old has gone, the new is here! (2 Corinthians 5:14-17)

Bear with each other and forgive one another if any of you has a grievance against someone. Forgive as the Lord forgave you. And over all these virtues put on love, which binds them all together in perfect unity. (Colossians 3:13,14)

This is how we know what love is: Jesus Christ laid down his life for us. And we ought to lay down our lives for our brothers and sisters. If anyone has material possessions and sees a brother or sister in need but has no pity on them, how can the love of God be in that person? Dear children, let us not love with words or speech but with actions and in truth. (1 John 3:16-18)

OBSERVATION

What is God saying to you? Write down a thought or truth that jumps out at you. What insight do you learn about love from these three passages?

APPLICATION

How can you apply these observations to your life today? How do you live in response to what you just read? Is there a spot where you get uncomfortable because of how God is calling you to live?

_____

_____

_____

_____

_____

_____

_____

PRAYER

Write a prayer about God's love in your life and your love for others.

_____

_____

_____

_____

_____

_____

_____

_____

_____

_____

PUT IT INTO PRACTICE

Do a chore for a family member without them asking.

— DAY 3 —
WHERE I'M STRONG: GOD WORKING THROUGH ME

> **A NEW COMMAND I GIVE YOU: LOVE ONE ANOTHER. AS I HAVE LOVED YOU, SO YOU MUST LOVE ONE ANOTHER. BY THIS EVERYONE WILL KNOW THAT YOU ARE MY DISCIPLES, IF YOU LOVE ONE ANOTHER.**
> John 13:34,35

A few moments after Jesus spoke these words, one of his friends betrayed him. A few hours later, the rest of his friends abandoned him, and one of his closest friends denied even knowing him. Not too long after that, he was whipped and beaten. In fewer than 24 hours, Jesus hung naked and bleeding on a cross while people mocked him. Still, he chose this moment to be a servant, to wash his disciples' feet, and to give them a command that would replace all the other rules that Jewish people were supposed to follow: *Love.* They were called to love one another in the same way Jesus loved them. And this would be the distinguishing mark of people who follow Jesus.

In which areas of your life has love come easily to you? In which areas have you learned how to love more? How do the people in your life know you are Jesus' disciple because of your love?

_____

_____

_____

_____

_____

ROOM FOR GROWTH: GOD WORKING IN ME

THEN WE WILL NO LONGER BE INFANTS, TOSSED BACK AND FORTH BY THE WAVES, AND BLOWN HERE AND THERE BY EVERY WIND OF TEACHING AND BY THE CUNNING AND CRAFTINESS OF PEOPLE IN THEIR DECEITFUL SCHEMING. INSTEAD, SPEAKING THE TRUTH IN LOVE, WE WILL GROW TO BECOME IN EVERY RESPECT THE MATURE BODY OF HIM WHO IS THE HEAD, THAT IS, CHRIST. FROM HIM THE WHOLE BODY, JOINED AND HELD TOGETHER BY EVERY SUPPORTING LIGAMENT, GROWS AND BUILDS ITSELF UP IN LOVE, AS EACH PART DOES ITS WORK.

Ephesians 4:14-16

Adulting is hard. Well, that's what my college-aged children say. As they get ready to tackle the responsibilities that come with independence, they realize adulthood isn't as magical as it might initially seem. However, to be a functioning adult, maturing isn't optional. Same with our faith. When in your life have you felt tossed back and forth by the voices in your own head, by other people, by the news and world events, by things that are not true?

_____

_____

_____

_____

_____

_____

_____

_____

_____

_____

_____

_____

_____

How can you—and the people around you who believe in Jesus—grow stronger together by using your gifts and loving others?

_____

_____

_____

_____

_____

_____

_____

_____

_____

_____

_____

PUT IT INTO PRACTICE
Take a meal to your child's teacher or a harried parent or your pastor's wife.

THRⱻE Rs MEDITATION

One of the teachers of the law came and heard them debating. Noticing that Jesus had given them a good answer, he asked him, "Of all the commandments, which is the most important?"

"The most important one," answered Jesus, "is this: 'Hear, O Israel: The Lord our God, the Lord is one. Love the Lord your God with all your heart and with all your soul and with all your mind and with all your strength.' The second is this: 'Love your neighbor as yourself.' There is no commandment greater than these."

"Well said, teacher," the man replied. "You are right in saying that God is one and there is no other but him. To love him with all your heart, with all your understanding and with all your strength, and to love your neighbor as yourself is more important than all burnt offerings and sacrifices."

Mark 12:28-33

After reading this, ask yourself these questions and write out your three Rs:

RⱻJOICE
What in this passage makes you praise God? What good news changes how you think and live?

_____

_____

_____

_____

_____

_____

_____

RePENT

What sin do you need to confess?

_____

_____

_____

_____

_____

_____

_____

ReQUEST

What do you want to ask God for?

_____

_____

_____

_____

_____

_____

_____

BONUS MEDITATION MoMENT

Memorize today's passage—or a portion of it. Say it out loud over and over again to help this truth sink in.

SEEING THE FRUIT DISPLAYED IN OTHERS

YOU, MY BROTHERS AND SISTERS, WERE CALLED TO
BE FREE. BUT DO NOT USE YOUR FREEDOM TO INDULGE
THE FLESH; RATHER, SERVE ONE ANOTHER HUMBLY IN LOVE.
FOR THE ENTIRE LAW IS FULFILLED IN KEEPING THIS ONE
COMMAND: "LOVE YOUR NEIGHBOR AS YOURSELF."

Galatians 5:13,14

LOVE MUST BE SINCERE. HATE WHAT IS EVIL;
CLING TO WHAT IS GOOD. BE DEVOTED TO ONE ANOTHER
IN LOVE. HONOR ONE ANOTHER ABOVE YOURSELVES.

Romans 12:9,10

Which people in your life humbly serve you? How do they honor you with their time, their words, their actions, their prayers? Write their names and the way they show love.

_____

_____

_____

_____

_____

_____

_____

_____

_____

_____

_____

_____

_____

_____

_____

_____

_____

_____

_____

_____

_____

_____

_____

_____

_____

_____

_____

_____

Next send a letter, email, or text—or make a phone call—to share your appreciation for how you see God's love working in their lives and through their lives.

IN YOUR OWN WORDS

"A friend of mine is amazing in that every so often he sends me a random text message thanking me for the work I do. I know it's a simple act, but the small show of appreciation goes so very far."

PRAYER PROMPTS

PRAYING TOGETHER

Dear Father, thank you for your eternal, faithful love to me. Dear Jesus, thank you for loving me so much that you were willing to leave heaven, come to earth, suffer, die, and rise again—all so I could be part of your family. Dear Spirit, work in me so that I love the Lord with all my heart, soul, mind, and strength and help me love my neighbors. Amen.

PRAYING PERSONALLY

Review the passages and your notes from this week. Choose one passage to reread, and then pray using ACTS:

ADORATION

What in this passage makes you adore God? What about his love is amazing to you? List those characteristics.

_____

_____

_____

_____

CONFESSION

What in this passage makes you aware of the times when your love is shallow?

_____

_____

_____

_____

_____

THANKSGIVING

What in this passage makes you thankful for God's love and for the love other people show you?

_____

_____

_____

_____

_____

_____

_____

_____

SUPPLICATION

Humbly and earnestly ask God to fill you with his love—and to help you pass along that love to others.

_____

_____

_____

_____

_____

_____

_____

_____

PUT IT INTO PRACTICE

Compliment someone who serves you.

JOY

THE FRUIT OF THE SPIRIT IS LOVE, JOY, PEACE, PATIENCE, KINDNESS, GOODNESS, FAITHFULNESS, GENTLENESS AND SELF-CONTROL.

Galatians 5:22,23

— DAY 1 —
DEVOTION

When you were in pre-K, you probably learned the song, "If You're Happy and You Know It (Clap Your Hands)." You dutifully clapped your hands, stomped your feet, and shouted, "Hurray!" Except . . . the older you got, the more you realized how easy it is to slap a fake smile on your face and pretend you're happy.

Life events—such as illness, divorce, recovery, addiction, or grieving—will place you in a season of struggle versus celebration. Perhaps world events leave you weighed down.

Maybe your addiction or illness clouds your spiritual view. Perhaps financial troubles or elected officials' decisions or depression fog you in. No matter what you see with your eyes, there is more to the story.

That's why the Bible doesn't list happiness as a fruit of the Spirit. Happiness is temporary and dependent on the circumstances or people around you. But *joy* is a display of the fruit of the Spirit. When King David was incredibly sad, he said, **"Hear, Lord, and be merciful to me; Lord, be my help. You turned my wailing into dancing; you removed my sackcloth and clothed me with joy, that my heart may sing your praises and not be silent. Lord my God, I will praise you forever"** (Psalm 30:10-12). That's when he found his joy.

God turns your crying into joy too. Even through hard times, you know you have someone who cares about you so much that he died for you. Someone who rose from the dead for you and sits next to God talking about you. Someone who is on your side—forever!

We can't see Jesus with our eyes right now, but people who did see him wrote Bible books about him. When troubles cloud around, friends who believe in Jesus remind us of things they can see clearly. These books written about Jesus remind us that Jesus gave up the glory of heaven to come to earth to save us. By living for us and taking God's punishment for us, he allows us to be called children of God. Now we have an eternity of cloudless, fogless peace waiting for us: **"Though you have not seen him, you love him; and even though you do not see him now, you believe in him and are filled with an inexpressible and glorious joy, for you are receiving the end result of your faith, the salvation of your souls"** (1 Peter 1:8,9).

SOAP MEDITATION

SCRIPTURE

These have come so that the proven genuineness of your faith—of greater worth than gold, which perishes even though refined by fire—may result in praise, glory and honor when Jesus Christ is revealed. Though you have not seen him, you love him; and even though you do not see him now, you believe in him and are filled with an inexpressible and glorious joy, for you are receiving the end result of your faith, the salvation of your souls. (1 Peter 1:7-9)

OBSERVATION

Write out the passage. What is one thing God is saying to you through it? Write down a thought or truth that jumps out at you. Is there a new insight for you?

_____

_____

_____

_____

_____

_____

_____

_____

_____

_____

_____

_____

_____

_____

APPLICATION

How can you apply that thought to your life today? How do you live in response to what you just read? Is there a spot where you get uncomfortable because of how God is calling you to live?

PRAYER

Write a prayer about this truth, and ask God for the strength to live it out.

WHERE I'M STRONG: GOD WORKING THROUGH ME

> I ALWAYS THANK MY GOD AS I REMEMBER YOU IN MY PRAYERS, BECAUSE I HEAR ABOUT YOUR LOVE FOR ALL HIS HOLY PEOPLE AND YOUR FAITH IN THE LORD JESUS. I PRAY THAT YOUR PARTNERSHIP WITH US IN THE FAITH MAY BE EFFECTIVE IN DEEPENING YOUR UNDERSTANDING OF EVERY GOOD THING WE SHARE FOR THE SAKE OF CHRIST. YOUR LOVE HAS GIVEN ME GREAT JOY AND ENCOURAGEMENT, BECAUSE YOU, BROTHER, HAVE REFRESHED THE HEARTS OF THE LORD'S PEOPLE.

Philemon 4-8

Imagine what it was like for Philemon to get this letter from the apostle Paul. I mean, really, Paul had persecuted Christians and then become a pillar of the church. Paul's a hero of faith, and he's telling Philemon that Philemon's love and encouragement is a refreshment?! How amazing to hear that!

Now imagine what it would be like for *you* to get that letter. How has your faith grown and deepened?

_____

_____

_____

_____

_____

_____

How has your love for God's holy people brought others great joy and encouragement?

_____

_____

_____

_____

_____

_____

_____

How have you refreshed the hearts of the Lord's people?

_____

_____

_____

_____

_____

_____

_____

_____

PUT IT INTO PRACTICE

When you put on your wedding ring, pray for your spouse. Or when you put on ANY ring, thank Jesus for being your Bridegroom.

— DAY 4 —
ROOM FOR GROWTH: GOD WORKING IN ME

THE WORD OF THE LORD SPREAD THROUGH THE
WHOLE REGION. BUT THE JEWISH LEADERS INCITED
THE GOD-FEARING WOMEN OF HIGH STANDING AND
THE LEADING MEN OF THE CITY. THEY STIRRED UP
PERSECUTION AGAINST PAUL AND BARNABAS,
AND EXPELLED THEM FROM THEIR REGION. SO THEY
SHOOK THE DUST OFF THEIR FEET AS A WARNING
TO THEM AND WENT TO ICONIUM. AND THE DISCIPLES
WERE FILLED WITH JOY AND WITH THE HOLY SPIRIT.

Acts 13:49-52

This passage is not exactly one that jumps out when it comes to talking about joy, is it? But it jumped out at me—and convicted me. Paul and Barnabas had just spent a whole bunch of time trying to share the joy of salvation with people in a city called Pisidian Antioch. They shared the good news in the synagogue (what we'd call a church today). The synagogue members invited them back for the next week's service. And the whole city came out. Pretty soon, the church leaders became jealous of Paul and Barnabas' popularity, but many people who weren't Jews started rejoicing. Then the leading (and popular) women and men of the city created a mob to torture Paul and Barnabas. There's a laundry list of reasons why the passage should end with: "And the disciples were discouraged, worn, and frustrated." But it didn't. They were filled with joy—and the Holy Spirit.

What struggles in your life leave you feeling discouraged, worn, and frustrated? How can you be filled with the Holy Spirit and celebrate with joy—even when it seems like people aren't listening to you, that they are against you and the work you are doing because of Jesus?

_____

_____

_____

_____

_____

_____

_____

_____

_____

_____

_____

_____

_____

_____

_____

_____

_____

_____

_____

_____

Important Note: Before you fill this out, please know that Solomon, the wisest man ever, said there is a time for everything, **"a time to weep and a time to laugh, a time to mourn and a time to dance"** (Ecclesiastes 3:4). If you are in a season where you are weeping and mourning, this may not be the time to do this exercise.

— DAY 5 —
THREE *R*s MEDITATION

> CONSIDER IT PURE JOY, MY BROTHERS
> AND SISTERS, WHENEVER YOU FACE
> TRIALS OF MANY KINDS, BECAUSE
> YOU KNOW THAT THE TESTING OF YOUR
> FAITH PRODUCES PERSEVERANCE.
>
> James 1:2,3

After reading this, ask yourself these questions and write out your three *R*s:

REJOICE
What in this passage makes you praise God? What good news changes how you think and live?

_____

_____

_____

_____

_____

_____

_____

_____

_____

_____

_____

RePENT

What sin do you need to confess?

_____

_____

_____

_____

_____

_____

_____

_____

ReQUEST

What do you want to ask God for?

_____

_____

_____

_____

_____

_____

_____

_____

BONUS MEDITATION MoMENT

Memorize today's passage—or a portion of it. Say it out loud over and over again to help this truth sink in.

SEEING THE FRUIT DISPLAYED IN OTHERS

I THANK MY GOD EVERY TIME I REMEMBER YOU.
IN ALL MY PRAYERS FOR ALL OF YOU, I ALWAYS
PRAY WITH JOY BECAUSE OF YOUR PARTNERSHIP
IN THE GOSPEL FROM THE FIRST DAY UNTIL NOW,
BEING CONFIDENT OF THIS, THAT HE WHO BEGAN
A GOOD WORK IN YOU WILL CARRY IT ON TO
COMPLETION UNTIL THE DAY OF CHRIST JESUS.

Philippians 1:3-6

Which people in your life pray with joy for the believers around them? How are they partners in the gospel, and how do they live their faith? Write their names and the way they bring others joy.

_____

_____

_____

_____

_____

_____

_____

_____

_____

_____

_____

_____

_____

_____

_____

_____

_____

_____

_____

_____

_____

_____

_____

_____

In the same way that Paul wrote to Philemon (on Day 3 this week), write (or text or email) to praise the people you listed. Maybe even paraphrase what Paul wrote to Philemon or what he wrote to the Philippians.

IN YOUR OWN WORDS
"A year ago, I put chocolate chip cookies in my neighbor's mailbox with my cell # after I saw an emergency vehicle drive away. She signs on to the Zoom Bible class I facilitate online every Tuesday. Joy!"

PRAYER PROMPTS

PRAYING TOGETHER

Dear Lord, your commands are right. They give joy to my heart and light to my eyes. Because of your salvation, I have an inexpressible and glorious joy. Help me pass along that joy to others and refresh the hearts of your people. Amen.

PRAYING PERSONALLY

Review the passages and your notes from this week. Choose one passage to reread, and then pray using ACTS:

ADORATION

What in this passage makes you adore God? What about his joy is amazing to you? List those characteristics.

_____

_____

_____

_____

_____

CONFESSION

When have you let this world steal your joy?

_____

_____

_____

_____

_____

_____

_____

THANKSGIVING

What in this passage makes you thankful for the joy God gives you?
Which joyful people in your life are you grateful for? List them all.

_____

_____

_____

_____

_____

_____

_____

_____

SUPPLICATION

Ask God to supply you with his joy and for you to bring that joy to
people who are hurting.

_____

_____

_____

_____

_____

_____

_____

_____

PEACE

THE FRUIT OF THE SPIRIT IS LOVE, JOY, PEACE,
PATIENCE, KINDNESS, GOODNESS, FAITHFULNESS,
GENTLENESS AND SELF-CONTROL.

Galatians 5:22,23

— DAY 1 —
DEVOTION

During the last dinner Jesus ate with his friends before he died, he knew their lives were about to get really hard. They would be laughed at, thrown in jail, mocked, beaten, and killed because of their faith in him and because they were telling more people about him.

So Jesus tried to give them a heads-up. He gave them a whole list of hard things, reminders, prayers, reassurances, and truth. Twice in five chapters of the Bible book of John—which is really one speech—he mentioned peace.

He told them, **"Peace I leave with you; my peace I give you. I do not give to you as the world gives. Do not let your hearts be troubled and do not be afraid"** (John 14:27). Later on he added, **"I have told you these things, so that in me you may have peace. In this world you will have trouble. But take heart! I have overcome the world"** (John 16:33).

You may not be persecuted and tortured, yet you also live in a broken world. You can pour out your questions to Jesus, say hard and honest things to him, tell him that your heart is broken and you don't know why. But after Jesus went to heaven, Paul shared a way for how to live with peace even in the middle of hard times: **"Do not be anxious about anything, but in every situation, by prayer and petition, with thanksgiving, present your requests to God. And the peace of God, which transcends all understanding, will guard your hearts and your minds in Christ Jesus"** (Philippians 4:6,7).

This is his promise: The God of heavenly armies stands guard over your heart and mind, shielding you with his inexplicable peace.

SOAP MEDITATION

We've already established that displaying the fruit of the Spirit is hard, right? So that means peace won't always be easy. Nowhere in the following passage does the psalmist say the word *peace*. He is wrestling with God as he struggles with sleepless nights. Even while meditating on God's words, he is troubled. Still, this psalm models what to do when peace is elusive. Maybe that's where you are at this point in your life. Maybe because of someone else's actions, peace has been a challenge. Maybe your own life choices leave you unsettled. Perhaps you wonder why God isn't just giving you peace.

Today as you meditate on this passage, notice that because peace doesn't magically happen, the psalmist simply recounts the times God was faithful because if God was faithful in the past, he would be faithful in the present and the future. Reviewing God's faithfulness can lead to trust, which leads to peace.

SCRIPTURE

I cried out to God for help; I cried out to God to hear me. When I was in distress, I sought the Lord; at night I stretched out untiring hands, and I would not be comforted. I remembered you, God, and I groaned; I meditated, and my spirit grew faint. You kept my eyes from closing; I was too troubled to speak. I thought about the former days, the years of long ago; I remembered my songs in the night. My heart meditated and my spirit asked: "Will the Lord reject forever? Will he never show his favor again? Has his unfailing love vanished forever? Has his promise failed for all time? Has God forgotten to be merciful? Has he in anger withheld his compassion?" Then I thought, "To this I will appeal: the years when the Most High stretched out his right hand. I will remember the deeds of the Lord; yes, I will remember your miracles of long ago. I will consider all your works and meditate on all your mighty deeds." Your ways, God, are holy. What god is as great as our God? You are the God who performs miracles; you display your power among the peoples. (Psalm 77:1-14)

OBSERVATION

What is one thing God is saying to you through this psalm? Write down a truth that jumps out at you. What new insight did you gain?

APPLICATION

How can you apply that thought to your life today? How do you live
in response to what you just read? When you are in a season of struggling, how can you use the psalmist's example to give you peace?

PRAYER

Write a prayer asking God to increase your peace.

_____

_____

_____

_____

_____

_____

_____

_____

_____

_____

_____

_____

_____

_____

_____

_____

_____

_____

_____

_____

_____

_____

PUT IT INTO PRACTICE

Ask a friend or church member how you can pray for them.

WHERE I'M STRONG: GOD WORKING THROUGH ME

> BUT THE WISDOM THAT COMES FROM HEAVEN IS FIRST OF ALL PURE; THEN PEACE-LOVING, CONSIDERATE, SUBMISSIVE, FULL OF MERCY AND GOOD FRUIT, IMPARTIAL AND SINCERE. PEACEMAKERS WHO SOW IN PEACE REAP A HARVEST OF RIGHTEOUSNESS.
>
> James 3:17,18

The older I get, the more wisdom I gain. After all, the experiences I've had show me that life is not just black and white. There is nuance, which leads to far less extreme reactions. In which areas of your life have you grown in wisdom?

_____

_____

_____

_____

_____

_____

_____

_____

_____

_____

How has this led to you becoming more peace-loving in your actions?

_____

_____

_____

_____

_____

_____

Where have you been able to harvest a righteous life because you've planted peace?

_____

_____

_____

_____

_____

_____

IN YOUR OWN WORDS

"When my husband and I were about to have our first child, members of our church invited us over for dinner. When we showed up, there was a table for two set in their living room. They served us a meal and let us enjoy a date night before we became a family of three. We paid it forward a few years later. My daughter's pre-K teacher was married to a man who was about to deploy. When they arrived at our house for dinner, my husband and I loaded up their two children and our three young children (5 kids 5 and under!) and we headed out to a restaurant. When we got back home to all have dinner together, they said it took them about 30 minutes to recover from the shock of a quiet evening all by themselves."

ROOM FOR GROWTH: GOD WORKING IN ME

FINALLY, BROTHERS AND SISTERS, REJOICE! STRIVE
FOR FULL RESTORATION, ENCOURAGE ONE ANOTHER,
BE OF ONE MIND, LIVE IN PEACE. AND THE GOD
OF LOVE AND PEACE WILL BE WITH YOU.

2 Corinthians 13:11

IF IT IS POSSIBLE, AS FAR AS IT DEPENDS ON YOU,
LIVE AT PEACE WITH EVERYONE.

Romans 12:18

Jesus came to earth to sacrifice his life—all so we could live at peace with the Father now and forever. Peace calls for sacrifice from people who call themselves Christians. Peace causes us to love others deeply, to serve them at our own expense, to comfort them, and to pass along grace. However, sometimes, no matter how hard we try, peace isn't possible.

What sacrifices might you have to make because of peace?

_____

_____

_____

_____

_____

_____

_____

How can you find peace knowing that sometimes peace isn't possible between you and everyone?

— DAY 5 —
THREE *R*s MEDITATION

Do not be anxious about anything, but in every situation, by prayer and petition, with thanksgiving, present your requests to God. And the peace of God, which transcends all understanding, will guard your hearts and your minds in Christ Jesus. Finally, brothers and sisters, whatever is true, whatever is noble, whatever is right, whatever is pure, whatever is lovely, whatever is admirable—if anything is excellent or praiseworthy—think [ponder, meditate] about such things. . . . And the God of peace will be with you."

Philippians 4:6-9

After reading this, write out your three *R*s:

ReJOICE
How can you praise God? What good news in this passage changes how you think and live?

_____

_____

_____

_____

_____

_____

_____

_____

_____

_____

REPENT

What sin do you need to confess?

_____

_____

_____

_____

_____

_____

_____

REQUEST

What can you ask God for?

_____

_____

_____

_____

_____

_____

_____

_____

_____

BONUS MEDITATION MOMENT

Memorize today's passage—or a portion of it. Say it out loud over and over again to help this truth sink in.

SEEING THE FRUIT DISPLAYED IN OTHERS

LET THE PEACE OF CHRIST RULE IN YOUR HEARTS,
SINCE AS MEMBERS OF ONE BODY YOU
WERE CALLED TO PEACE. AND BE THANKFUL.

Colossians 3:15

AND THE PEACE OF GOD, WHICH TRANSCENDS
ALL UNDERSTANDING, WILL GUARD YOUR
HEARTS AND YOUR MINDS IN CHRIST JESUS.

Philippians 4:7

Think about people in your life who exude peace through their everyday interactions. Have they modeled that they have God's peace, a peace that doesn't make sense? How do they show that this peace guards their hearts and minds? Write about those people and the examples they set for you.

_____

_____

_____

_____

_____

_____

_____

_____

_____

_____

_____

_____

_____

_____

_____

_____

_____

_____

_____

_____

_____

_____

_____

_____

_____

_____

_____

_____

_____

Today, send a letter, email, or text—or make a phone call—to share your appreciation for how you see God's peace guarding their hearts and minds and how that carries over into how they live.

PRAYER PROMPTS

PRAYING TOGETHER

Dear Spirit, continue to remind me of the truth that peace—thanks to Jesus giving me peace with the Father—is standing guard over my heart and mind. Protect my thoughts and emotions from the roller-coaster events of this world that might tempt me to lose focus. Give me the strength to model this peace and to lead others to want to know how to find this peace for themselves. Then give me the right words to talk about the only real, lasting peace. Amen.

PRAYING PERSONALLY

Review the passages and your notes from this week. Choose one passage to reread, and then pray using ACTS:

ADORATION

What in this passage makes you adore God? What about his peace is amazing to you? List those characteristics.

_____

_____

_____

_____

_____

_____

_____

_____

_____

_____

_____

CONFESSION

What in this passage makes you aware of your lack of peace?

_____

_____

_____

_____

_____

THANKSGIVING

What in this passage makes you thankful?

_____

_____

_____

_____

SUPPLICATION

Humbly and earnestly ask God to supply everything you and the people you love and the strangers around the world need—including peace with God and peace with each other.

_____

_____

_____

_____

PUT IT INTO PRACTICE

Donate to a food bank.

PATIENCE

THE FRUIT OF THE SPIRIT IS LOVE, JOY, PEACE, PATIENCE, KINDNESS, GOODNESS, FAITHFULNESS, GENTLENESS AND SELF-CONTROL.

Galatians 5:22,23

— DAY 1 —
DEVOTION

When my kids were little, they had all the patience of, well, pre-K students. My mom would constantly remind them to slow down, to wait, to be patient. They heard that reminder so often that soon all she had to say was, "What's Grandma's word?" They'd reply with a sigh, exaggerating the two syllables: "Pay-shence."

They were learning from a young age how to wait without throwing a tantrum. (Well, it worked for Grandma. They reserved some tantrums for me.) As adults, we're pretty familiar with impatience too. We want relationship issues reconciled quickly, illnesses healed immediately, and crises resolved rapidly. And we want Jesus to come back ASAP. The joke is that you shouldn't pray for patience because he won't just give it to you; he'll teach it to you—and that's a hard lesson.

When we picture patience, we often imagine a grandma who doesn't mind when the kids break the eggs and spill the flour while baking, as if patience is sweet and gentle. But patience is far harder. It requires perseverance and develops the quality of being long-suffering. It often feels more like you've gone through Navy SEAL training and endured Hell Week. In this worst week of training, candidates spend five and a half sleepless days constantly working, cold, hungry, wet, and dirty—all while getting yelled at. It's so brutal that 70 to 80 percent quit.

As much as you might want to, life doesn't let you quit, does it? You can't just stop dealing with the sudden death of your spouse, the addiction that grips your adult child, the depression that darkens your days, the health struggles of your elderly parents, the 24/7 requirements of your medically fragile middle schooler.

Jesus' brother James phrases it well: **"Blessed is the one who perseveres under trial because, having stood the test, that person will receive the crown of life that the Lord has promised to those who love him"** (James 1:12). His wording reminds you that patience is not weakness; it is strength. It comes from the confidence that God will keep all his promises, that your future is going to be way better than your past, and that God is managing all the events of your life to get you to the finish line with your faith intact. **"Wait for the Lord; be strong and take heart and wait for the Lord!"** (Psalm 27:14). What's God's Word? *Patience!*

— DAY 2 —
SOAP MEDITATION

SCRIPTURE

We continually ask God to fill you with the knowledge of his will through all the wisdom and understanding that the Spirit gives, so that you may live a life worthy of the Lord and please him in every way: bearing fruit in every good work, growing in the knowledge of God, being strengthened with all power according to his glorious might so that you may have great endurance and patience, and giving joyful thanks to the Father, who has qualified you to share in the inheritance of his holy people in the kingdom of light. For he has rescued us from the dominion of darkness and brought us into the kingdom of the Son he loves, in whom we have redemption, the forgiveness of sins. (Colossians 1:9-14)

OBSERVATION

Write out the portion of this passage that jumps out at you about patience. Is there a new insight you learned?

_____

_____

_____

_____

_____

_____

_____

_____

_____

_____

_____

APPLICATION

How can you apply that thought to your life today? How do you live in response to what you just read? Did anything make you uncomfortable about the times you may not have been patient? Is there a situation where God is teaching you patience?

PRAYER

Write a prayer about patience, and ask God for the strength to live it out.

_____

_____

_____

_____

_____

_____

_____

_____

_____

_____

_____

_____

_____

_____

_____

_____

_____

_____

_____

_____

PUT IT INTO PRACTICE

Pay it forward with a cup of coffee or at a drive-through.

— DAY 3 —
WHERE I'M STRONG: GOD WORKING THROUGH ME

A PERSON'S WISDOM YIELDS PATIENCE; IT IS TO ONE'S GLORY TO OVERLOOK AN OFFENSE.

Proverbs 19:11

It doesn't necessarily feel glorified to keep your mouth shut, does it? I mean, social media's "success" comes not from calm, rational discussion but instead from highlighting offenses. This is not the life to which you've been called. Write down how you see your wisdom being expressed as patience. How have you overlooked offenses honestly— not passive aggressively?

_____

_____

_____

_____

_____

_____

_____

_____

_____

_____

_____

_____

_____

_____

_____

_____

_____

_____

_____

_____

_____

_____

_____

_____

_____

_____

_____

_____

PUT IT INTO PRACTICE

Start a home group. A great way to get closer to people and to learn more about Jesus is to meet regularly. Whether you choose once a month or once a week, open your home or meet at a coffee shop or brewery to read a little bit of the Bible and talk about it.

— DAY 4 —

ROOM FOR GROWTH: GOD WORKING IN ME

BUT FOR THAT VERY REASON I WAS SHOWN
MERCY SO THAT IN ME, THE WORST OF SINNERS,
CHRIST JESUS MIGHT DISPLAY HIS IMMENSE
PATIENCE AS AN EXAMPLE FOR THOSE WHO WOULD
BELIEVE IN HIM AND RECEIVE ETERNAL LIFE.

1 Timothy 1:16

The apostle Paul said he was the worst of sinners, and God used him to show just how patient God is. You know how much you sin—and how much your forgiveness and joy in God's grace can be an example for others. Is there a person in your life who needs your patience, even when you'd rather give up on them?

_____

_____

_____

_____

_____

_____

_____

_____

_____

IN YOUR OWN WORDS

"You can go on walks with a friend and truly listen."

THREE Rs MEDITATION

But do not forget this one thing, dear friends: With the Lord a day is like a thousand years, and a thousand years are like a day. The Lord is not slow in keeping his promise, as some understand slowness. Instead he is patient with you, not wanting anyone to perish, but everyone to come to repentance. So then, dear friends, since you are looking forward to this, make every effort to be found spotless, blameless and at peace with him. Bear in mind that our Lord's patience means salvation, just as our dear brother Paul also wrote you with the wisdom that God gave him.

2 Peter 3:8,9,14,15

After reading this, write out your three Rs:

REJOICE
How can you praise God?

_____

_____

_____

_____

_____

_____

_____

_____

_____

_____

_____

_____

RePENT
What sin do you need to confess?

_____

_____

_____

_____

_____

_____

_____

_____

ReQUEST
What can you ask God for?

_____

_____

_____

_____

_____

_____

_____

BONUS MEDITATION MOMENT
Memorize today's passage—or a portion of it. Say it out loud over and over again to help this truth sink in.

— DAY 6 —

SEEING THE FRUIT DISPLAYED IN OTHERS

> WE DO NOT WANT YOU TO BECOME LAZY, BUT TO IMITATE THOSE WHO THROUGH FAITH AND PATIENCE INHERIT WHAT HAS BEEN PROMISED.
>
> Hebrews 6:12

Think about which people in your life have been examples of faith and patience? How has their example led you to imitate them?

_____

_____

_____

_____

_____

_____

_____

_____

_____

_____

_____

After writing out that example, contact them to share your thanks for how you see God working in them and through them.

PRAYER PROMPTS

PRAYING TOGETHER

Dear Father, you are so patient with me. Every day I do the sins I don't want to do, and you keep forgiving me. Use me and my thankfulness for your patience to talk to others about your patience with them. Use the trials you allow in my life to develop patience in me so I am patient with others. Amen.

PRAYING PERSONALLY

Review the passages and your notes from this week. Choose one passage to reread, and then pray using ACTS:

ADORATION

What in this passage makes you adore God? Is it his power or his compassion, his truth or his grace? List those characteristics.

_____

_____

_____

_____

_____

CONFESSION

What in this passage makes you aware of your lack of patience? God already knows about the times you were impatient, but it is good for you to admit them.

_____

_____

_____

_____

_____

THANKSGIVING

What in this passage makes you thankful for God's patience with you? List everything!

_____

_____

_____

_____

_____

_____

_____

_____

_____

SUPPLICATION

Humbly and earnestly ask God to supply everything you and the people you love and the strangers around the world need—including patience.

_____

_____

_____

_____

_____

_____

_____

_____

_____

KINDNESS

THE FRUIT OF THE SPIRIT IS LOVE, JOY, PEACE,
PATIENCE, KINDNESS, GOODNESS, FAITHFULNESS,
GENTLENESS AND SELF-CONTROL.

Galatians 5:22,23

— DAY 1 —
DEVOTION

Deep down, people want a modern-day definition of karma to be the standard operating procedure for how the world works. We want good to happen to "good" people, and we want "bad" people to get what's coming to them.

God's standard operating procedure couldn't be more different. His whole nature is expressed by his perfect Son taking the punishment for the guilty people—and the guilty people getting the credit for the Son's perfection. Our minds can't wrap around that kind of kindness, but it does lead us to look at life differently: **"Make sure that nobody pays back wrong for wrong, but always strive to do what is good for each other and for everyone else"** (1 Thessalonians 5:15).

Kindness gives you the strength to be kind to the people who have different political opinions or lifestyles or to people who don't know Jesus. Kindness allows you to live out the love of Jesus with the people around you: your family, friends, coworkers, and strangers. Kindness means that when one part of the Christian family hurts, you hurt with it. Kindness also gives you the motivation to speak the truth in love even (and especially) when it's hard.

There's some advice in the Bible for wives who are married to men who don't believe in Jesus: **"If any of them do not believe the word, they may be won over without words by the behavior of their wives, when they see the purity and reverence of your lives"** (1 Peter 3:1,2). Every believer can apply that. We will never argue people into the kingdom, but we can love them, speak God's Word, and let the Holy Spirit bring them into the kingdom. People will know we are Christians by our love—not because we're jerks.

True kindness means karma doesn't stand a chance.

— DAY 2 —
SOAP MEDITATION

SCRIPTURE
Therefore, as we have opportunity, let us do good to all people, especially to those who belong to the family of believers. (Galatians 6:10)

Get rid of all bitterness, rage and anger, brawling and slander, along with every form of malice. Be kind and compassionate to one another, forgiving each other, just as in Christ God forgave you. (Ephesians 4:31,32)

Anxiety weighs down the heart, but a kind word cheers it up. (Proverbs 12:25)

Whoever oppresses the poor shows contempt for their Maker, but whoever is kind to the needy honors God. (Proverbs 14:31)

OBSERVATION
Which of those four passages catches your attention most? Write out that passage. Then write down a thought or truth that jumps out at you. Is there a new insight you learned?

_____

_____

_____

_____

_____

_____

_____

_____

_____

_____

_____

APPLICATION

How can you apply these passages to your life today? In what areas of your life are you kind? Where can you see the opportunity to express even more kindness? Is there a spot where you get uncomfortable because of how God is calling you to live?

PRAYER
Write a prayer about this truth, and ask God for the strength to live it out.

_____

_____

_____

_____

_____

_____

_____

_____

_____

_____

_____

_____

_____

_____

_____

_____

_____

_____

_____

PUT IT INTO PRACTICE
As you drive by the places where your children go to school or work, pray for them to be faithful students or employees; ask God to bless their teachers and employers.

WHERE I'M STRONG: GOD WORKING THROUGH ME

God raised us up with Christ and seated us with him in the heavenly realms in Christ Jesus, in order that in the coming ages he might show the incomparable riches of his grace, expressed in his kindness to us in Christ Jesus. For it is by grace you have been saved, through faith—and this is not from yourselves, it is the gift of God—not by works, so that no one can boast. For we are God's handiwork, created in Christ Jesus to do good works, which God prepared in advance for us to do.

Ephesians 2:6-10

The best part of the fruit of the Spirit is knowing that for each act you carry out, God thought of it first. He formed you exactly how you are to be a blessing to the people around you—and you are!

In which areas of your life have you been kind to people, doing the good works that God prepared in advance for you to do? How have you been clothed with Jesus and then clothed yourself with his qualities?

_____

_____

_____

_____

_____

_____

_____

_____

_____

_____

_____

_____

_____

_____

_____

_____

_____

_____

_____

_____

_____

_____

_____

_____

_____

IN YOUR OWN WORDS

"Being real. Being vulnerable. Sharing either the personal 'rooster crowing' moments and God's evident grace afterward. When others share these moments, it encourages me to share mine. It shows realness and struggle. People need to know they are not alone or not too far from God for him to love them. Sometimes when someone comments on how strong my faith may seem, I'll share my less-than moments. It's not about me, but I feel it reflects the true love of God and that despite my horrific weaknesses and faults, I'm still (by God's grace) not afraid to cling to him."

ROOM FOR GROWTH: GOD WORKING IN ME

THEREFORE, AS GOD'S CHOSEN PEOPLE, HOLY AND
DEARLY LOVED, CLOTHE YOURSELVES WITH COMPASSION,
KINDNESS, HUMILITY, GENTLENESS AND PATIENCE.
BEAR WITH EACH OTHER AND FORGIVE ONE ANOTHER
IF ANY OF YOU HAS A GRIEVANCE AGAINST SOMEONE.
FORGIVE AS THE LORD FORGAVE YOU.

Colossians 3:12,13

You were made by God and formed by him; you are his handiwork. Sometimes, though, the temptation to tamp down the Holy Spirit inside of you is strong because you want to do what comes naturally— which can often be putting yourself first.

How can you grow in bearing with other people and forgiving them? Where can you grow in clothing yourself with God's qualities?

_____

_____

_____

_____

_____

_____

_____

_____

_____

_____

What people in your life seem unkind? How can you be kind to them?

— DAY 5 —
THReE *Rs* MEDITATION

It's easy to confuse nice with kind. Psalm 141 clears that up. Kindness doesn't always feel good. Sometimes kind means saying the hard yet necessary things that need to be said.

> DO NOT LET MY HEART BE DRAWN TO WHAT IS EVIL SO THAT I TAKE PART IN WICKED DEEDS ALONG WITH THOSE WHO ARE EVILDOERS; DO NOT LET ME EAT THEIR DELICACIES. LET A RIGHTEOUS MAN STRIKE ME—THAT IS A KINDNESS; LET HIM REBUKE ME—THAT IS OIL ON MY HEAD. MY HEAD WILL NOT REFUSE IT, FOR MY PRAYER WILL STILL BE AGAINST THE DEEDS OF EVILDOERS.

Psalm 141:4-6

After reading this psalm, write out your three *R*s:

ReJOICE
How can you praise God? What good news in this psalm changes how you think and live?

_____

_____

_____

_____

_____

_____

_____

_____

RePENT
What sin do you need to confess?

_____

_____

_____

_____

_____

_____

_____

_____

ReQUEST
What can you ask God for?

_____

_____

_____

_____

_____

_____

_____

_____

BONUS MEDITATION MoMENT
Memorize today's passage—or a portion of it. Say it out loud over and over again to help this truth sink in.

— DAY 6 —

SEEING THE FRUIT DISPLAYED IN OTHERS

> ONCE SAFELY ON SHORE, WE FOUND OUT
> THAT THE ISLAND WAS CALLED MALTA.
> THE ISLANDERS SHOWED US UNUSUAL KINDNESS.
> THEY BUILT A FIRE AND WELCOMED US ALL
> BECAUSE IT WAS RAINING AND COLD.
>
> Acts 28:1,2

This is kind of a weird passage, isn't it? Paul was in a shipwreck, and everyone reached land safely. Once there, the people of Malta "showed unusual kindness" simply by welcoming them, warming them, and drying them out. In the middle of hard times, the simplest of gestures can seem unusually kind. What people in your life reflected God's love in tangible ways during your hard times?

After writing out those examples, reach out to them to thank them. They may not even know that what they did made such an impact on you.

PRAYER PROMPTS

PRAYING TOGETHER

Sometimes, Holy Spirit, what you ask me to do is hard. That's why I can't be kind without you. Thank you for living inside of me, for filling me with the strength and intention to live kindly, to do the good deeds prepared for me to do. Work in me so that I also extend kindness by saying the hard truths that need to be said with love. And help me to receive others' hard, kind words with grace. Amen.

PRAYING PERSONALLY

Review the passages and your notes from this week. Choose one passage to reread, and then pray using ACTS:

ADORATION

What in this passage makes you adore God? What about God's kindness is astonishing to you? List those characteristics.

_____

_____

_____

_____

_____

_____

_____

_____

_____

_____

_____

_____

CONFESSION

What in this passage makes you aware of your lack of kindness?

_____

_____

_____

_____

_____

_____

_____

_____

THANKSGIVING

What in this passage makes you thankful for God's kindness to you? What about other people's kindness to you makes you thankful? How does being kind to others make you feel thankful?

_____

_____

_____

_____

_____

_____

_____

_____

_____

_____

SUPPLICATION

Humbly and earnestly ask God to supply you with extra kindness.

_____

_____

_____

_____

_____

_____

_____

_____

_____

_____

_____

_____

_____

_____

_____

_____

_____

PUT IT INTO PRACTICE

While waiting at a stoplight, ask God to stop Satan's attacks, to have more patience, or to stop your family from falling into temptation.

GOODNESS

THE FRUIT OF THE SPIRIT IS LOVE, JOY, PEACE, PATIENCE, KINDNESS, GOODNESS, FAITHFULNESS, GENTLENESS AND SELF-CONTROL.

Galatians 5:22,23

— DAY 1 —
DEVOTION

Bloodhounds have such a sensitive sense of smell that they can distinguish smells at least a thousand times better than humans. Some bloodhounds have been known to stick to a trail for more than 130 miles. These dogs are such reliable trackers that their evidence is admissible in a court of law. When King David said, **"Surely your goodness and love will follow me all the days of my life, and I will dwell in the house of the Lord forever"** (Psalm 23:6), he was really saying that God's goodness will hound you. You can't run away from God's goodness; it's inescapable. When Jesus came down from heaven to track you down with his love (which is more than 130 miles), he brought peace with God. The blessings in your life aren't random. They aren't accidents or luck. You don't stumble around and accidentally find them. It's all intentional: **"May the God of hope fill you with all joy and peace as you trust in him, so that you may overflow with hope by the power of the Holy Spirit. I myself am convinced, my brothers and sisters, that you yourselves are full of goodness"** (Romans 15:13,14).

Every day you get to take the goodness you've been given and pass it on to others, until the day you meet Jesus face-to-face. That's when you'll hear him say: **"Well done, good and faithful servant! You have been faithful with a few things; I will put you in charge of many things. Come and share your master's happiness!"** (Matthew 25:23,24).

PUT IT INTO PRACTICE
When you open social media in the morning, pray for the first person whose post you see.

— DAY 2 —

SOAP MEDITATION

SCRIPTURE

His divine power has given us everything we need for a godly life through our knowledge of him who called us by his own glory and goodness. Through these he has given us his very great and precious promises, so that through them you may participate in the divine nature, having escaped the corruption in the world caused by evil desires. For this very reason, make every effort to add to your faith goodness; and to goodness, knowledge; and to knowledge, self-control; and to self-control, perseverance; and to perseverance, godliness; and to godliness, mutual affection; and to mutual affection, love. For if you possess these qualities in increasing measure, they will keep you from being ineffective and unproductive in your knowledge of our Lord Jesus Christ. But whoever does not have them is nearsighted and blind, forgetting that they have been cleansed from their past sins. (2 Peter 1:3-9)

OBSERVATION

What is one thing that God is saying to you through this section of his Word? There's a lot to digest here, so rewrite the portion of this section that jumps out at you. (Or write out the whole passage.) Is there a new insight you learned?

APPLICATION

How can you apply that thought to your life today? How do you live in response to what you just read? Is there a spot where you get uncomfortable because of how God is calling you to live?

_____

_____

_____

_____

_____

_____

_____

PRAYER

Write a prayer about this truth, and ask God to possess these qualities in increasing measure.

_____

_____

_____

_____

_____

_____

_____

PUT IT INTO PRACTICE

Take a meal to someone who is sick or lonely or recovering from surgery or just had a baby. Can't leave the house? Give them a gift card to a restaurant that delivers.

WHERE I'M STRONG: GOD WORKING THROUGH ME

> WITH THIS IN MIND, WE CONSTANTLY PRAY FOR YOU, THAT OUR GOD MAY MAKE YOU WORTHY OF HIS CALLING, AND THAT BY HIS POWER HE MAY BRING TO FRUITION YOUR EVERY DESIRE FOR GOODNESS AND YOUR EVERY DEED PROMPTED BY FAITH.
>
> 2 Thessalonians 1:11

Paul, Silas, and Timothy wrote to the members of God's family who lived in a city called Thessalonica. In the very beginning of the letter, they praised those people for how much their faith was growing and how their love for each other was increasing. Your faith is growing and your love for others is increasing too. God's power is at work in you. Through your faith in him, list five good deeds you carried out that were a blessing to others.

_____

_____

_____

_____

_____

_____

_____

_____

ROOM FOR GROWTH: GOD WORKING IN ME

FOR YOU WERE ONCE DARKNESS, BUT NOW YOU
ARE LIGHT IN THE LORD. LIVE AS CHILDREN OF LIGHT
(FOR THE FRUIT OF THE LIGHT CONSISTS IN ALL
GOODNESS, RIGHTEOUSNESS, AND TRUTH)
AND FIND OUT WHAT PLEASES THE LORD.

Ephesians 5:8-10

It's easy to live for ourselves. Well, speaking for myself it is. But that doesn't please the Lord. Being a child of the light calls for something different. It calls for loving goodness, righteousness, and truth, which are not mutually exclusive. What aspects of your life still tempt you to think darkness is better than light?

_____

_____

_____

_____

_____

_____

_____

_____

_____

_____

_____

How can you show goodness and truth this week?

_____

_____

_____

_____

_____

_____

_____

_____

_____

_____

_____

_____

_____

_____

IN YOUR OWN WORDS

"After I had heart surgery, I had to take mandatory supervised walks immediately after being brought to the ICU. My nurse came on duty, and she had to take four walks with me that shift. During and after every ten-minute walk, she'd compliment something—my slippers, my balance, my increased 'speed,' or my smile. Sure made me want to walk instead of making me feel I HAD to walk. Now I like to compliment others too, but I don't get out much. So I try to compliment my coworkers more often."

THREE Rs MEDITATION

> I REMAIN CONFIDENT OF THIS:
> I WILL SEE THE GOODNESS OF THE LORD
> IN THE LAND OF THE LIVING.
>
> Psalm 27:13

After reading this, write out your three Rs:

ReJOICE

How can you praise God? What good news in this psalm changes how you think and live?

_____

_____

_____

_____

_____

_____

_____

_____

_____

_____

_____

_____

_____

RePENT
What sin do you need to confess?

_____

_____

_____

_____

_____

_____

_____

ReQUEST
What can you ask God for?

_____

_____

_____

_____

_____

_____

_____

BONUS MEDITATION MoMENT
Memorize today's passage—or a portion of it. Say it out loud over and over again to help this truth sink in.

SEEING THE FRUIT DISPLAYED IN OTHERS

THEREFORE, AS WE HAVE OPPORTUNITY, LET US
DO GOOD TO ALL PEOPLE, ESPECIALLY TO THOSE
WHO BELONG TO THE FAMILY OF BELIEVERS.

Galatians 6:10

MAY THE GOD OF HOPE FILL YOU WITH ALL
JOY AND PEACE AS YOU TRUST IN HIM, SO THAT
YOU MAY OVERFLOW WITH HOPE BY THE POWER
OF THE HOLY SPIRIT. I MYSELF AM CONVINCED,
MY BROTHERS AND SISTERS, THAT YOU YOURSELVES
ARE FULL OF GOODNESS, FILLED WITH KNOWLEDGE
AND COMPETENT TO INSTRUCT ONE ANOTHER.

Romans 15:13,14

Which people in your life are full of goodness and knowledge? How do they help mentor you in your life of faith?

_____

_____

_____

_____

_____

_____

_____

_____

_____

_____

_____

_____

_____

_____

_____

_____

_____

_____

_____

_____

_____

_____

_____

_____

_____

_____

_____

_____

_____

After writing out those examples, let them know. Send a letter, email, or text—or even make a phone call. Share your thanks for how you see God's goodness in them.

PRAYER PROMPTS

PRAYING TOGETHER
Dear God, it's still overwhelming to me that you and your goodness chased me down—and continue to follow me. Thank you! Help me shine my light and overflow that goodness to the people around me. Amen.

PRAYING PERSONALLY
Review the passages and your notes from this week. Choose one passage to reread, and then pray using ACTS:

ADORATION
What in this passage makes you adore God? What about his goodness astonishes you? List those characteristics.

_____

_____

_____

_____

_____

CONFESSION
What in this passage makes you aware of the times you don't overflow with God's goodness?

_____

_____

_____

_____

_____

_____

_____

THANKSGIVING

What in the passage you chose makes you thankful?

_____

_____

_____

_____

_____

_____

_____

SUPPLICATION

Ask God to remind you of his goodness, and then share that goodness with others. What other people and issues are on your heart that need to see God's goodness?

_____

_____

_____

_____

_____

_____

_____

_____

_____

FAITHFULNESS

THE FRUIT OF THE SPIRIT IS LOVE, JOY, PEACE,
PATIENCE, KINDNESS, GOODNESS, FAITHFULNESS,
GENTLENESS AND SELF-CONTROL.

Galatians 5:22,23

DEVOTION

Hurricane Irma hit Florida in 2017. Torrential rain and 107 mph winds pounded the state. As one homeowner took shelter, she looked out her bathroom window and saw a Muscovy duck sitting on a nest of 13 eggs. The duck endured the first round of the hurricane, stayed on the nest during the calm eye of the storm, and weathered the second round, getting covered in broken branches and Spanish moss. Twenty-four hours later, Irma (as the homeowner named her) finally left her nest; all the eggs were still intact.

What a good picture of our God's faithfulness. **"Surely he will save you from the fowler's snare and from the deadly pestilence. He will cover you with his feathers, and under his wings you will find refuge; his faithfulness will be your shield and rampart"** (Psalm 91:3,4).

Jesus refused to abandon the storm of the Father's wrath, remaining on the cross and covering us with his blood. Thanks to him, we have a Father who will never abandon us as we weather life's storms—temptation, illness, accidents, loneliness, death, divorce, financial struggles. God promises that whatever struggles we face, he is our shelter, our peace, our protection. Even after the storms have passed, he stays with us. Because that's what our Father does.

Because of the Father's faithfulness to us, we are faithful to him and to others—a legacy of faith that comes from being part of God's family. When Paul wrote a letter to a man named Philemon, he shared: **"I always thank my God when I mention you in my prayers because I hear about your faithfulness to the Lord Jesus and your love for all of God's people. As you share the faith you have in common with others, I pray that you may come to have a complete knowledge of every blessing we have in Christ. Your love for God's people gives me a lot of joy and encouragement. You, brother, have comforted God's people"** (Philemon 4-7 GW).

This is what faithfulness looks like: sharing your faith; learning more about the blessings that come from being part of Christ's family; loving the Christian family; and bringing joy, encouragement, and comfort to the people around you.

— DAY 2 —
SOAP MEDITATION

SCRIPTURE
Hebrews 11:1-40. Normally I wouldn't have you meditate on almost a thousand words, but this section seems pertinent to the topic of faithfulness. We don't know who wrote the book of Hebrews, but the anonymous author took the time to mention individuals and groups of people whose faith led them to lead lives of faithfulness—even in the middle of life's storms. Today, please open your Bible—whether a book or an app—and read all of Hebrews chapter 11.

OBSERVATION
Write down a thought or truth that jumps out at you. Is there a new insight here for you? Which example of faith—and faithfulness—stands out?

_____

_____

_____

_____

_____

APPLICATION
How do you live in response to what you just read? How does it give you joy or encouragement? Is there a spot where you get uncomfortable because of how God is calling you to live?

_____

_____

_____

_____

PRAYER

Write a prayer about faithfulness, and ask God for the strength to live it out.

PUT IT INTO PRACTICE

As you look at the stars in the sky, pray for God to help you keep your eyes on heaven, thank him for keeping his promises, and praise him for how immense his creation is.

WHERE I'M STRONG:
GOD WORKING THROUGH ME

I always thank my God when I mention you in my prayers because I hear about your faithfulness to the Lord Jesus and your love for all of God's people. As you share the faith you have in common with others, I pray that you may come to have a complete knowledge of every blessing we have in Christ. Your love for God's people gives me a lot of joy and encouragement. You, brother, have comforted God's people.

Philemon 4-7 GW

In Yellowstone National Park, you'll find a geyser called Old Faithful. Its eruptions have been tracked for so long that National Park Service employees can now predict—in a ten-minute window—when the next eruption will occur. Old Faithful got its name simply because it regularly, consistently does what it was made to do.

You are God's Old Faithful. Because you have a complete knowledge of every blessing Christ gives you, you then faithfully erupt with encouragement, comfort, joy, and love. People can predict it because that's what you do.

Yesterday we looked at Hebrews chapter 11 and a whole list of people who were faithful. If your name was added to the list for generations of believers to read, what might it say? Write it out.

By faith <fill in your name> . . . then list how you have lived by faith.

_____ _____

_____ _____

_____

_____

ROOM FOR GROWTH: GOD WORKING IN ME

The end of all things is near. Therefore be alert and of sober mind so that you may pray. Above all, love each other deeply, because love covers over a multitude of sins. Offer hospitality to one another without grumbling. Each of you should use whatever gift you have received to serve others, as faithful stewards of God's grace in its various forms. If anyone speaks, they should do so as one who speaks the very words of God. If anyone serves, they should do so with the strength God provides, so that in all things God may be praised through Jesus Christ. To him be the glory and the power for ever and ever. Amen.

1 Peter 4:7-11

How have you not used the gifts God gave you to serve him and others faithfully? In what area of your life might you need some focus on being faithful, building you up to be more effective and productive in your faithfulness?

_____

_____

_____

_____

_____

_____

_____

_____

_____

_____

_____

This is not meant to guilt you but to create a moment of honest confession. Write out your confession and then pray.

_____   _____

_____

_____

_____

_____

_____

_____

_____

_____

_____

_____

_____

_____

_____

_____

_____

_____

_____

PUT IT INTO PRACTICE
Do a prayer walk in your neighborhood and invite people to join you.

THREE *R*s MEDITATION

Therefore, brothers and sisters, since we have confidence to enter the Most Holy Place by the blood of Jesus, by a new and living way opened for us through the curtain, that is, his body, and since we have a great priest over the house of God, let us draw near to God with a sincere heart and with the full assurance that faith brings, having our hearts sprinkled to cleanse us from a guilty conscience and having our bodies washed with pure water. Let us hold unswervingly to the hope we profess, for he who promised is faithful. And let us consider how we may spur one another on toward love and good deeds, not giving up meeting together, as some are in the habit of doing, but encouraging one another—and all the more as you see the Day approaching.

Hebrews 10:19-25

After reading this, write out your three *R*s:

REJOICE
How can you praise God?

_____

_____

_____

_____

_____

_____

_____

_____

_____

_____

REPENT
What sin do you need to confess?

_____

_____

_____

_____

_____

_____

_____

_____

REQUEST
What can you ask God for?

_____

_____

_____

_____

_____

_____

_____

BONUS MEDITATION MOMENT
Memorize today's passage—or a portion of it. Say it out loud over and over again to help this truth sink in.

— DAY 6 —
SEEING THE FRUIT DISPLAYED IN OTHERS

DEAR FRIEND, I PRAY THAT YOU MAY ENJOY GOOD
HEALTH AND THAT ALL MAY GO WELL WITH YOU,
EVEN AS YOUR SOUL IS GETTING ALONG WELL. IT GAVE
ME GREAT JOY WHEN SOME BELIEVERS CAME AND
TESTIFIED ABOUT YOUR FAITHFULNESS TO THE TRUTH,
TELLING HOW YOU CONTINUE TO WALK IN IT.

3 John 2-3

Think about people in your life who display God's faithfulness through their everyday interactions. How have they reflected God's love in tangible ways?

_____

_____

_____

_____

_____

_____

_____

After writing out that example, send a letter, email, or text—or even make a phone call. Share your thanks for how you see God working in them.

PRAYER PROMPTS

PRAYING TOGETHER

Dear Father, thank you for guarding me with your faithfulness and protecting me from the enemy. Thank you also for sharing example after example of other believers' faithfulness, which encourages me to continue that legacy of faithfulness to the people around me. And thank you for the ultimate promise you give that if I am faithful until I die, you will give me the crown of life. Amen.

PRAYING PERSONALLY

Review the passages and your notes from this week. Choose one passage to reread, and then pray using ACTS:

ADORATION

What in this passage makes you adore God? What about his faithfulness amazes you? List his awesome characteristics and simply tell him.

_____

_____

_____

_____

CONFESSION

What in the passage makes you aware of your sins? God already knows that you did them, but it is good to admit to the big ones and share the little ones—and apologize for ones you don't even know about.

_____

_____

_____

_____

THANKSGIVING

What things in this reading make you grateful?

_____

_____

_____

_____

_____

_____

_____

SUPPLICATION

Humbly and earnestly ask God to supply everything you and the people you love and the strangers around the world need—for faithfulness and for life.

_____

_____

_____

_____

_____

_____

_____

PUT IT INTO PRACTICE

Donate stuffed animals to the local police or sheriff departments. Officers often carry them in their trunks in case they meet a child involved in an accident.

GENTLENESS

THE FRUIT OF THE SPIRIT IS LOVE, JOY, PEACE, PATIENCE, KINDNESS, GOODNESS, FAITHFULNESS, GENTLENESS AND SELF-CONTROL.

Galatians 5:22,23

— DAY 1 —
DEVOTION

In a matter of seconds, I found these comments on the Internet:

"Shut your mouth; you are so disrespectful."

"Your tiny brain just can't handle it."

"Come on, guys, let's start boxing and punching him in the face."

"How old are you, kid? Where did you learn to speak in such a mewling yet accusatory tone?"

I bet you've read similar—or worse—things. We've probably all said similar—or worse—things too. The phrase "sticks and stones may break my bones, but words will never hurt me" is a lie. The truth is that **"the words of the reckless pierce like swords, but the tongue of the wise brings healing"** (Proverbs 12:18).

This is one of the reasons that the Holy Spirit wants you to display gentleness. If you are trying to tell people about their Savior, yelling at them, calling them names, or putting them down for their horrible decisions isn't going to help them believe that God's family is a great place to be. That's why God says, **"Opponents must be gently instructed, in the hope that God will grant them repentance leading them to a knowledge of the truth, and that they will come to their senses and escape from the trap of the devil, who has taken them captive to do his will"** (2 Timothy 2:25,26).

Your gentleness is one way God will bring people to learn about him— to bring eternal healing!

PUT IT INTO PRACTICE
Call a friend. Ask questions. Listen. Check in.

— DAY 2 —
SOAP MEDITATION

SCRIPTURE

Remind the people to be subject to rulers and authorities, to be obedient, to be ready to do whatever is good, to slander no one, to be peaceable and considerate, and always to be gentle toward everyone. At one time we too were foolish, disobedient, deceived and enslaved by all kinds of passions and pleasures. We lived in malice and envy, being hated and hating one another. But when the kindness and love of God our Savior appeared, he saved us, not because of righteous things we had done, but because of his mercy. He saved us through the washing of rebirth and renewal by the Holy Spirit, whom he poured out on us generously through Jesus Christ our Savior, so that, having been justified by his grace, we might become heirs having the hope of eternal life. This is a trustworthy saying. And I want you to stress these things, so that those who have trusted in God may be careful to devote themselves to doing what is good. These things are excellent and profitable for everyone. (Titus 3:1-8)

OBSERVATION

Write out the passage. What is one thing that God is saying to you through it? Write down a thought or truth that jumps out at you. Is there a new insight for you?

_____

_____

_____

_____

_____

_____

_____

_____

APPLICATION

How can you apply that thought to your life today? How do you live in response to what you just read? Is there a spot where you get uncomfortable because of how God is calling you to live?

_____

_____

_____

_____

_____

_____

_____

_____

PRAYER

Write a prayer asking for God to work in you, to make gentleness your default setting.

_____

_____

_____

_____

_____

_____

_____

_____

WHERE I'M STRONG: GOD WORKING THROUGH ME

> THEREFORE, AS GOD'S CHOSEN PEOPLE, HOLY AND DEARLY LOVED, CLOTHE YOURSELVES WITH COMPASSION, KINDNESS, HUMILITY, GENTLENESS AND PATIENCE.
>
> Colossians 3:12

Because you are clothed with Christ, you get to clothe yourself with his qualities. Write down an area where you were clothed with Jesus' gentleness and shared that with someone else recently. In which areas of your life have you been gentle? How have you shown restraint?

_____

_____

_____

_____

_____

_____

_____

_____

_____

_____

_____

_____

_____

_____

_____

_____

_____

_____

_____

_____

_____

_____

_____

_____

_____

_____

_____

_____

_____

_____

PUT IT INTO PRACTICE

Speak up about mistakes, failings, and sin—and then forgive. (This is more for me personally, but maybe it will help you too.) Healthy relationships also require hard conversations. If you're struggling with someone close to you, let him or her know. If you see a fellow believer in Jesus making life choices that aren't compatible with his will, put the friend above the friendship and talk to him or her.

ROOM FOR GROWTH: GOD WORKING IN ME

A GENTLE ANSWER TURNS AWAY WRATH,
BUT A HARSH WORD STIRS UP ANGER.

Proverbs 15:1

THROUGH PATIENCE A RULER CAN BE PERSUADED,
AND A GENTLE TONGUE CAN BREAK A BONE.

Proverbs 25:15

In which areas of your life have you not been gentle? What changes in your life would help you be more gentle?

_____

_____

_____

_____

_____

_____

_____

_____

_____

_____

_____

_____

_____

Today's passages help us consider how the peace we have from God expresses itself in how we act toward others. How have you seen your words stir up anger?

_____

_____

_____

_____

_____

_____

_____

_____

_____

_____

Is there a person in your life who needs your gentleness, even if it's really hard?

_____

_____

_____

_____

_____

_____

_____

_____

_____

THREE *R*s MEDITATION

EVERYONE SHOULD BE QUICK TO LISTEN,
SLOW TO SPEAK AND SLOW TO BECOME ANGRY,
BECAUSE HUMAN ANGER DOES NOT PRODUCE
THE RIGHTEOUSNESS THAT GOD DESIRES.

James 1:19,20

REJOICE IN THE LORD ALWAYS. I WILL SAY
IT AGAIN: REJOICE! LET YOUR GENTLENESS BE
EVIDENT TO ALL. THE LORD IS NEAR.

Philippians 4:4,5

After reading these passages, write out your three *R*s:

REJOICE
How can you praise God?

_____

_____

_____

_____

_____

_____

_____

_____

_____

RePENT

What sin do you need to confess?

_____

_____

_____

_____

_____

_____

_____

_____

ReQUEST

What can you ask God for?

_____

_____

_____

_____

_____

_____

_____

_____

BONUS MEDITATION MoMENT

Memorize today's passage—or a portion of it. Say it out loud over and over again to help this truth sink in.

SEEING THE FRUIT DISPLAYED IN OTHERS

> BUT IN YOUR HEARTS REVERE CHRIST AS LORD. ALWAYS BE PREPARED TO GIVE AN ANSWER TO EVERYONE WHO ASKS YOU TO GIVE THE REASON FOR THE HOPE THAT YOU HAVE. BUT DO THIS WITH GENTLENESS AND RESPECT.
>
> 1 Peter 3:15

What people in your life share the hope that they have gently and respectfully? Write about those people and the examples set for you.

_____

_____

_____

_____

_____

_____

_____

_____

_____

Send a letter, email, or text—or make a phone call—to share your appreciation for how you see God working in their lives.

PRAYER PROMPTS

PRAYING TOGETHER

Dear Spirit, work in me so that my words bring healing, that my responses are gentle, and that you control my tongue. Forgive the times I stir up anger. Help me instead respond with gentleness and respect. Amen.

PRAYING PERSONALLY

Review the passages and your notes from this week. Choose one passage to reread, and then pray using ACTS:

ADORATION

What in this passage makes you adore God? What about his gentleness to you is amazing? List those characteristics.

_____

_____

_____

_____

_____

_____

CONFESSION

Where do you need to confess your lack of gentleness?

_____

_____

_____

_____

_____

_____

THANKSGIVING

What in this passage makes you thankful?

_____

_____

_____

_____

_____

_____

_____

_____

SUPPLICATION

Pray for God to fill you with his gentleness and to supply the world with gentleness.

_____

_____

_____

_____

_____

_____

_____

_____

_____

SELF-CONTROL

THE FRUIT OF THE SPIRIT IS LOVE, JOY, PEACE,
PATIENCE, KINDNESS, GOODNESS, FAITHFULNESS,
GENTLENESS AND SELF-CONTROL.

Galatians 5:22,23

— DAY 1 —
DEVOTION

Self-control is not popular.

You will often hear the current advice to "follow your heart" or "do what you love." Well, from what God tells us, the truth is that **"out of the heart come evil thoughts—murder, adultery, sexual immorality, theft, false testimony, slander"** (Matthew 15:19). So following our hearts often means that we'll be self-centered rather than self-controlled.

Christians aren't great at talking about self-control either. I don't think I've seen a popular word art sign or T-shirt that reads, "Deny Yourself!" Yet from what God tells us, **"Whoever wants to be my disciple must deny themselves and take up their cross and follow me"** (Matthew 16:24).

Left to our own devices, we prefer self-centeredness over self-control because it's easier to coast through the day doing what comes naturally.

However . . . that's not what we've been called to do. We've been called not to blow the budget on impulsive buys, not to have one drink turn into three, not to use our words to hurt other people and their reputations. The challenge is that we don't have a self-created, unending well of self-control—but here's where we can get it: **"The grace of God . . . teaches us to say 'No' to ungodliness and worldly passions, and to live self-controlled, upright and godly lives in this present age"** (Titus 2:11,12).

You and I can't develop self-control by being self-reliant. Instead, we look outside ourselves to God's unconditional love and let that grace flow through us.

— DAY 2 —
SOAP MEDITATION

SCRIPTURE

For this reason I remind you to fan into flame the gift of God, which is in you through the laying on of my hands. For the Spirit God gave us does not make us timid, but gives us power, love and self-discipline. So do not be ashamed of the testimony about our Lord or of me his prisoner. Rather, join with me in suffering for the gospel, by the power of God. He has saved us and called us to a holy life—not because of anything we have done but because of his own purpose and grace. This grace was given us in Christ Jesus before the beginning of time, but it has now been revealed through the appearing of our Savior, Christ Jesus, who has destroyed death and has brought life and immortality to light through the gospel. (2 Timothy 1:6-10)

OBSERVATION

Which portion of this passage stands out to you about self-control? Is there a new insight for you?

_____

_____

_____

_____

_____

_____

_____

_____

_____

_____

_____

APPLICATION

How can you apply that thought to your life today? How do you live in response to what you just read? Does anything make you uncomfortable regarding how God has called you to live?

_____

_____

_____

_____

_____

_____

PRAYER

Write a prayer about self-control, and ask God for the strength to live it out.

_____

_____

_____

_____

_____

_____

_____

_____

PUT IT INTO PRACTICE

Go a day with no complaining.

WHERE I'M STRONG: GOD WORKING THROUGH ME

> **FOR THE SPIRIT GOD GAVE US DOES NOT MAKE US TIMID, BUT GIVES US POWER, LOVE AND SELF-DISCIPLINE.**
>
> 2 Timothy 1:7

In which areas of your life have you been powerfully full of self-control? Over the course of your life, how have you developed more self-control?

_____

_____

_____

_____

_____

_____

_____

_____

_____

PUT IT INTO PRACTICE

Speak a blessing over your children. My husband has a habit of blessing the kids before he goes to bed. He'll stand over their beds or outside their doors or just say it as he hugs them goodnight because sometimes they're up later than we are now. He might change it slightly, but for the most part he uses the words from Numbers 6:24-26: "The LORD bless you and keep you; the LORD make his face shine on you and be gracious to you; the LORD turn his face toward you and give you peace."

— DAY 4 —
ROOM FOR GROWTH: GOD WORKING IN ME

LIKE A CITY WHOSE WALLS ARE BROKEN THROUGH IS A PERSON WHO LACKS SELF-CONTROL.

Proverbs 25:28

The Great Wall of China is enormous, which is why it's not called the Mediocre Wall of China. While the United States measures approximately 3,000 miles from east to west, the Great Wall is 13,170 miles long. To protect citizens from enemies, an ancient city needed strong, *complete* walls. The problem, however, is that the Great Wall isn't actually one wall. It's simply sections of walls that aren't necessarily connected—some are parallel, and some are in sections all by themselves. This is why Genghis Kahn was able to invade the country a thousand years ago and slaughter citizens.

You need a protective wall too for your heart, mind, and soul. And you have one! At your baptism, the Holy Spirit came to live inside of you, giving you a spiritual wall that protects you from your enemies. Where have you allowed your enemy to break through your walls?

_____

_____

_____

_____

_____

_____

_____

THReE *R*s MEDITATION

For the grace of God has appeared that offers salvation to all people. It teaches us to say "No" to ungodliness and worldly passions, and to live self-controlled, upright and godly lives in this present age, while we wait for the blessed hope—the appearing of the glory of our great God and Savior, Jesus Christ, who gave himself for us to redeem us from all wickedness and to purify for himself a people that are his very own, eager to do what is good.

Titus 2:11-14

After reading this, write out your three *R*s:

ReJOICE

How can you praise God? What good news here changes how you think and live?

_____

_____

_____

_____

_____

_____

_____

_____

_____

_____

_____

REPENT
What sin do you need to confess?

_____

_____

_____

_____

_____

_____

_____

REQUEST
What can you ask God for?

_____

_____

_____

_____

_____

_____

_____

BONUS MEDITATION MOMENT
Memorize today's passage—or a portion of it. Say it out loud over and over again to help this truth sink in.

SEEING THE FRUIT DISPLAYED IN OTHERS

THEREFORE ENCOURAGE ONE ANOTHER AND BUILD EACH
OTHER UP, JUST AS IN FACT YOU ARE DOING. NOW WE
ASK YOU, BROTHERS AND SISTERS, TO ACKNOWLEDGE
THOSE WHO WORK HARD AMONG YOU, WHO CARE
FOR YOU IN THE LORD AND WHO ADMONISH YOU.

1 Thessalonians 5:11,12

Think about people in your life who have encouraged you to exhibit self-control through their everyday interactions. How have they reflected God's love in tangible ways? How have they had hard conversations with you, reminding you that self-indulgence won't actually lead to the life God desires for you?

_____

_____

_____

_____

_____

_____

_____

_____

After writing out those examples, let them know. Send a letter, email, or text—or even make a phone call. Share your thanks for how you see God working in them to encourage you.

PRAYER PROMPTS

PRAYING TOGETHER

Dear Jesus, thank you for offering salvation to all people. Father, thank you for your grace, which teaches me to say no to ungodliness and worldly passions. Spirit, rule in me so that I lead a self-controlled, upright, and godly life while I wait for Jesus Christ and that his mercy makes me eager to do what is good. Amen.

PRAYING PERSONALLY

Review the passages and your notes from this week. Choose one passage to reread, and then pray using ACTS:

ADORATION

What in this passage makes you adore God? Is it his power or his compassion, his truth or his grace? List those characteristics.

CONFESSION

What in this passage makes you aware of your lack of self-control? God already knows that you struggle with this at times, but it is good for you to admit it.

_____

_____

_____

_____

_____

THANKSGIVING

What in this passage makes you thankful? List everything!

_____

_____

_____

_____

_____

SUPPLICATION

Humbly and earnestly ask God to supply everything you and the people you love and the strangers around the world need—including self-control.

_____

_____

_____

_____

_____

ABOUT THe WRITER

Linda Buxa is a freelance communications professional as well as a regular blogger and contributing writer for Time of Grace Ministry. Linda is the author of *Dig In! Family Devotions to Feed Your Faith*, *Parenting by Prayer*, and *Made for Friendship*. She and her husband, Greg, have lived in Alaska, Washington D.C., and California. After retiring from the military, they moved to Wisconsin, where they settled on 11.7 acres and now keep track of 15 chickens, multiple cats, and 1 black Lab. Their 3 children insist on getting older and following their dreams, so Greg and Linda are rapidly approaching the empty-nest stage. The sign in her kitchen sums up their lives: "You call it chaos; we call it family."

ABOUT TIME OF GRACE

Time of Grace is an independent, donor-funded ministry that connects people to God's grace—his love, glory, and power—so they realize the temporary things of life don't satisfy. What brings satisfaction is knowing that because Jesus lived, died, and rose for all of us, we have access to the eternal God—right now and forever.

To discover more, please visit timeofgrace.org or call 800.661.3311.

HELP SHARE GOD'S MESSAGE OF GRACE

Every gift you give helps Time of Grace reach people around the world with the good news of Jesus. Your generosity and prayer support take the gospel of grace to others through our ministry outreach and help them experience a satisfied life as they see God all around them.

Give today at timeofgrace.org/give or by calling 800.661.3311.

Thank you!